Daniel St Amour

The polar bear testament

Without religion

Lemelin — Cooper

Credits:

Illustration: Robert Émile Fortin, artist painter (December 19th 1945 – July 8th 2004)

Infographics: Luc Jacques. & Anne-Marie Jacques

First revision: Danny Doo
Linguistic revision: Micheline Harvey
English traduction: Danny Doo

Daniel St Amour
186, rue Houle App 1
St Eustache, Qc. Canada.

Email: groupeinvisible@videotron.ca

ISBN 978-2-9815531-2-6 (Paper)
ISBN 978-2-9815531-3-3 (PDF)
ISBN 978-2-9815531-4-0 (E-PUB)
Original title 2012: Sans religions, le testament de l'ours polaire.

Prologue

Why entitle this book *"whit out religion"*? After years of reflexion and meditation on my too long life and also on the many different teachings that I had the privilege to receive from my enlightened friends and also from their god whom they talk all the time… you know that god? That invisible god which many people talk frequently about, and seemingly no one have never seen? I have decided to write here the essential stories of their life. They gave me hope of a better world, more enlightened, and most of all, a world more in peace with itself. Without those exceptional humans I would of never have found the country of my birth, the paradise of my childhood. It is in their memory that I transmit to you everything that I have learned from them.

The polar bear.

Once upon a time, there was a bear who lived in a country called the polar artic. This country was made of snow and ice and it was very cold. A lot of the animals who lived in these spaces were covered with long silky hair, and others had bald smooth skin with inside of them layers of grease to protect them from the cold.

There were also beings called humans, who had to hunt the animals to feed themselves and make cloths out of their skin to survive. In this country there was no sound except for the wind that blew all day. Sometimes the wind was gentile and caressed our faces with tenderness and affection, but in other times, the wind was so violent that we had to protect ourselves from it. For all beings that lived in this country, this place was called paradise, and it really was.

There was in this paradise, a legend. This legend was one of a polar bear who seemingly had more than thirteen thousand years and had the capacity to communicate with humans, and sometimes, to savagely behave like them, like wild beast.

The polar legend lived away from the other bears because he didn't speak like them either. The polar bears from the ice fields caught him many times speaking and talking to himself. He repeated often the same things by howling these words in the wind: « Were ever you are, I thank you all, and I will always love you ».

The other polar bears asked him many times why was he howling these words into thin air? He repeated endlessly the same old stories of humans that he had known while living amongst them. Extraordinary humans who had change the face of the earth. The other bears questioned themselves if he wasn't little bit crazy, because for them, the world they always had known, was made of water, ice and cold. As far away they could remember, the world they knew was always been like this.

They talk about him between themselves; they called him the crazy one. The legendary polar bear knew that, but he couldn't care less, it amused him and even made him laugh. He loved the other polar bears after all. He profoundly loved them, because he was like them, happy to live amongst them. He was a polar bear.

The odyssey of the little penguin

The legend was known from all the animals around the planet. One day, at the other end of earth, in Antarctica, a little penguin heard one of the stories of the legendary polar bear and decided to go search for him. All the other penguins strongly advised him not to go over the Ice Mountains that give them protection and also the ocean that gave them food. So the little penguin decided to stay, and to fear like the others to go over what was known from all. Every day, the only thing the little penguin could think about was the bear and its legend; he could not believe that such an animal could exist. He wanted to meet him, wished to see him with his own eyes, ear him with his own ears. Every time he talked to his siblings about the legendary bear, they all firmly advised him not to, telling him: « Don't go over of what is known or you will die and wander for eternity».

The little penguin was scandalized and raged against his pears; He didn't believe what they were telling him. He was firmly decided to meet the bear;

he had the courageous foolishness. Knowing that he would never get the approbation from the others he decided, against all, to leave them and search for the legend. He brought some fish that he attached on his back, took a deep breath, stamped the snow under his legs and started walking in the direction of the mountains protecting the universe of the penguins.

After a few days, while he was marching into the unknown, he doubted of his quest for the legendary bear. He taught that maybe he should have listened to the others, maybe he should have tried to convince some of his friends to accompany him. What will happen of him on the other side of the mountains, of the ocean? He doubted... but his desires to know if the legendary polar bear really existed, was far much stronger than his doubts.

Eight days after his departure, he arrived at the feet of the mountains. Impressed, he asks himself how he would climb it. He looked at his little feet and implored them: « Please, don't let me down, I need you more than ever. For the moment, I will lie down, eat, and sleep. Tomorrow, I will ask you to help me climb the impossible all the way to the unknown. If this can reassure you my little legs, I am also scared! ». When he waked up, the little penguin was full of energy and confident. He looked at his little feet and saw that they had some frost bites, but no more. He stood up, stretched, and went. He started ascending the mountain. He didn't look back or forward. He concentrated only on his feet. He taught of all the reasons that brought him here. He counted on his feet, and they also counted on him, in this perilous adventure in which he dragged them. Seconds after seconds, minutes after minutes, hour after hour, he climbed relentlessly the unknown, didn't see the time passing, like it never existed.   Suddenly, he felt his little legs shaking. After a moment, he had to stop. Exhausted and out of breath, he fell to sleep in an instant. He past the two following days sleeping. He dreamt of his friends and family, of the penguin's reunions and banquets full of fish of all kinds. In his dream he was happy and joy full. The little penguin opened his eyes slowly and noticed that the sun was glorious and heated his body and help him get rid of his frost bites. He looked around and only saw the horizon. He laughed, yelled, and dance: He was at the top of the mountain! He could see far away, the country of the penguins, and at the other side, the reflection of the unknown ocean. He had climbed the impossible!

He turned all his attention at the unknown, the thing that always scared the other penguins. He look as far has he could to see if there was any monster hiding somewhere. He didn't see darkness either, or anything scary that the others told him. He asks himself were these beliefs come from; why the other penguins feared the unknown? He didn't understand, because from his point of view, the sun was shining on both sides: the known and the unknown. The little penguin hate the last fishes that was left, hate some snow that he left melted in his mouth to quench his thirst, and let the last bite fell in his stomach. He stood up, looked all the way down and started the descent of the mountain. When he arrived at the ocean, he saw far away a family of wales of his acquaintance. He wave at them by agitating his wings and Yelled:

— Hey ho! My friends!

Intrigued, the wales approached him. The little penguin expressed his desire to go to the North Pole to find a polar bear. The wales looked at him perplexed. The oldest one of the group asked him:

— Little penguin, how will you get to the North Pole? Do you only know where this place is?

—No! I don't know where the North Pole is. That is the reason why I called you. I know that you are all great travellers. Your stories of adventures in unknown seas are legendary in the country of the penguins. Can you help me to get there?

The wales consulted each other and after a moment they all agreed by shaking their heads up and down in sign of approbation. The oldest one responds:

—Little penguin, we will take you half way, and by the same occasion we will profit from this trip to meet our cousins that we didn't see for many moons. When we get there, we will ask some of them who travels frequently to the North Pole to bring you there.

The little penguin jumped joyfully: Chance was on his side. He rushed to jump on the back of the mammal and they all swam parading to the north.

After a few weeks, they arrived at destination. The wales were happy to find their cousins. They feast many days, telling each other's crazy stories and anecdotes of their childhood. The wales from the South Pole talked to their cousins of the north the desire of the little penguin to travel to the artic. A few of them volunteered to accompany him and also to profit from the months of sunshine of the north hemisphere. Moons after, the little penguin and his new friends swam to the country of the white bears.

After a few weeks of swimming, they cross the path of icebergs, drifting at the will of the wind and tides. When they arrived near the ice fields, the little penguin jumped into the water, saluting the wales that plunged in the deep cold water sea. He walked many days, getting deeper and deeper in the ice fields. He looked at the horizon, wishing to see another animal that could help him find the legendary bear. He started to be impatient and once again doubted of his quest. The hungriness hurt his belly. He had hated all his provisions and started to panic: « I don't know where the sea and its fish are! »

Suddenly, he remembered what the other penguin had told him: « Don't go over of what is known or you will die and wander for eternity ».

« What did I do? I was stupid and stubborn. I should have never left the country of the penguins! »

He looked far away into the unknown with tears in his eyes. He didn't know what he had to do anymore. His body and spirit were exhausted; he fell asleep under the weight of his tears and torments. Waking up, all of his face was ice frozen. The cold and wind had glued his tears onto his face; some of them had formed ice pics on the corner of his puffy and swollen eyes. Raging against himself, he painfully unhooked them from his face, examined them and ate them. « I won't let you the pleasure of reminding me my stubbornness and stupidity. Maybe it is true that I am lost for ever, but whatever happens, I will pursue my crazy quest! »

He continued to walk forward with uncertainty and anxiety still raging against himself. While walking, he kicked the snow and ruminated against his siblings. « Why didn't you stop me from doing this foolishness? Why I didn't listen to you? » He continued his path furiously.

One day, at the rising sun, he observed the surroundings to try and find the nourishing sea. His little belly couldn't take it anymore. Suddenly, he saw far away, mounds of snow that seemed to move.

« What is this? He taught. Moving snow? I have to see this more closely! »

Curious, he walked towards these moving snow balls. He was stupefied. He never saw anything like this in his life! Far away he shouted:

— Hey you! Over there! The moving snow balls, wait for me! I come from the country of the penguins and I am starving! Please, I need help… I am lost… wait for me!

The snow balls were now coming to him. He shouted even more:

— Hey you… hey you!

Seeing that he wouldn't be alone anymore, he felt a great relief. He founded back his hope; he was saved. He got closer to these things that he had saw far away and started to take shape. He now saw legs, noses, and mouth armed with long teeth's. He heard some growling's that made him trembling with terror.

« Oh! These things don't seem that friendly, they growl like my hungry belly ».

The hope that he had found back for a brief moment, transformed into fear and great menace. Worrying that his life could be in danger, he turned back and ran as fast than his legs could. Looking back, he noticed that he would never succeed to lose them, that it was a lost cause that he would never escape from them. Maybe it would be better to accept the inevitable and finish his quest into the stomach of one of these enormous beasts of an immaculate white.

Suddenly, He stopped and turned too looked at these hungry beasts. He raised his eyes toward the sky and started to pray loudly:

— Father of all penguins, great artist of life, I put my life under your wings. I thank you for everything. I am now ready to meet you in paradise.

At the end of his prayer, he kneeled down and bows his head in sign of submission in front of the eternal. He continued to pray waiting for a certain death, and open his little eyes in direction of the white monsters. They all had stopped, and looked at him with fear. The little penguin swept his tears from his face and shouted:

— What are you waiting for? I am ready to be devoured. I am ready to die!

He looked at them, paralysed, and taught:

« What is wrong? Why don't they attack me?

He suddenly felt a breath on his neck that made him tremble in terror… he imagined the worst. He turned back slowly and was nose to nose with one of these monsters which sniffed him from head to toes. The little penguin started to pray again with more conviction: Penguin in the sky, pardon my foolishness. The only thing I desired was to meet the legendary polar bear. To see him with my own eyes, and ear stories from his own mouth.

On these words, the white monster smiled at him and said:

— Little penguin, your wishes and prayer have been granted: I am the bear that you were looking for.

The little penguin could not believe his ears. Speechless, he strutted:

— You… you are… the legendary bear? That is what a polar bear looks like?

— Say what! You were searching for me and you didn't know what a polar bear looked like!

— No! I had no idea.

— Little penguin, you are crazy and I like you. For a moment, they looked at each other without any words. The little penguin broke the silence:

— I have something to ask you.

— What can I do for you?

— Could you ask the other bears behind me not to eat me right now?

— What other bears?

The little penguin turned his head and saw the other bears walking away from them.

— Why did they left? I was ready to be eaten and die.

— Because they fear me. Most of them think that I am crazy, and because of that they won't dare to confront me… they believe that I am capable of the worst horrors.

— They fear you? But you seem so gentile. I can smell you with my nose and you smell nice and soft.

— I smell nice and soft? You make me laugh little penguin of my dreams! You warm my heart. It has been a long time since I heard that kind of thing… I have to tell you that you also smell soft.

Both of them started to laugh. The fear of the little penguin had disappeared. He wouldn't end his life in the stomach of one of these bears. More than that, he had realized his quest: The legendary polar bear was in front of him, laughing heartily with him. He had so many questions to ask him that he didn't know where to start. He risked another question:

— Bear, I heard so many things from you in my country! Now that you are in front of me, I am speechless. I have heard that you were thirteen thousands years old and some centuries, and that you have lived amongst the savage humans.

— This is the truth; I effectively have thirteen thousands years old and some centuries, and yes, I lived amongst the savage humans… like you say.

— But how can that be possible?

— It is a long story… if you really want to know, I will tell you everything of my life amongst humans and how everything began.

— Yes! Please tell me all! This is why I came here. I want to know everything of you.

— But before I start telling my stories little penguin, what do you say if we left this place?

— I approve, but don't walk to fast, because my legs are shorts and tired.

— I have an idea, mount on my back and I will tell you one of my stories.

— Me? Ride on the back of the legendary polar bear? You are serious? Super!

On these words, the polar bear kneeled down, and the penguin rushed to mount on the back of his new friend. They both left with a smile on their face, happy to be together. The little penguin was still amazed of meeting with the legend. He had difficulty to believe he had found the legendary bear, and adding to that, he was riding on his back. He taught that no penguins from his country would believe him. While they were walking, the bear turned his head to look at his new friend and said:

— Penguin of my dreams, I am happy to have found you, I am disposed to answer all your questions.

— Why do you call me penguin of your dreams?

— It is because I dreamt of you while I was asleep. I was receiving images of a white and black animal that was praying. I didn't know what these images were corresponding to. I had this dream for seven days. This morning, when I woke up, I heard a voice saying: « Go to the south of the icefield, there is a little penguin that needs you. » Does this answer your question?

— A voice told you to come and find me?

— Yes! But this voice that I have heard came from my belly, from my guts.

— Do you hear this voice often?

— From time to time. Whenever I hear this voice, it is because someone out there needs my help, I let this voice guide me. This voice is soft spoken and loving, like a warm loving murmur. Is there something else you wish to know?

— Oh yes! Tell me everything. I want to know everything of you and wish that you start from the beginning of your incredible life.

— Ok then. For your pleasure and mine, I will tell you how everything started. About thirteen thousand and some centuries ago, some humans from a faraway country came and abduct me while I was just a little cub. They ran after me and I got stroked with an object they had in their hands in such a manner that I couldn't move. All of my body was numb from head to toe. I couldn't escape. They putted me in a cage and drag me on a vehicle that had the particularity to slide on snow. I saw my mother and father crying out of rage against these humans. I was their only son and talk about me to the other polar bears with joy and proudness. I was a great loss for them. Sometime after, the humans stopped and grabbed my cage, and transported me on a vessel that seemed to float on water.

— Oh yes! I have seen these vessels while I was travelling on the back of the wales.

— So you have a good idea what I am talking about. Little penguin, permit me to continue my story. So I was transported inside this floating vessel. A few weeks later, the vessel accost on the land of a country that I knew nothing about. They brought me food that I didn't hate or taste. Then they putted me in a cage, a much bigger cage, in which there was other cubs like me. In this prison, we had all: snow, ice and a little lake with fish in it. It looked like my country, but smaller.

— This is incredible! Weren't you afraid?

— Yes, I was very afraid. I didn't understood why I was there, and I cried all the tears of my body. I sob so much. I wished I had my parents with me. Slowly but surely, I approached the others and made some friends. Sometimes we cried together.

— There is something that I don't understand. Why these humans have abducted you from your country and then to put you in a cage?

— To expose us to the other humans, you understand? There were other animals in this place which got abducted just like me. They came from strange countries, different than ours. This place where we were all locked up was called a zoo.

— Since you can talk with humans, couldn't you tell them to free you, to take you back to your parents?

— In these times, I was incapable to communicate with the humans. This faculty was given to me many years later.

— I believed that you always had this capacity, that is what also believes all the penguins.

— No, that is not quite true. You really want to know how I got that faculty. You really want to know?

—Oh yes! Tell me.

— Ok then, here it is! After living seventeen years in a cage doing nothing more than to eat, swim and sleep, in which we were all used to live in. An individual with a white mane like mine, came and open the zoo big door to free us. We were all there looking at each other confused. This human entered and looked at us, one after the other. He pointed his finger at me and made a sign with his hand to follow him.

— You want to hear what follows, little penguin?

— Yes! Please continue!

— Ok then, I will pursue…

The white mane man

Noah

Have you ever heard of this man named Noah? Do you know what he did for the animals? Did you know that this man really existed? It is because of him and his invisible god if I am still alive today and that I can testify of the authenticity of this humble and magnificent person; a simple but courageous being without any sparks, to whom a divine mission had been confide. Do you know why this man had been chosen amongst millions of others to execute this mission? It is because this man secretly vowed in his heart an unconditional love to this invisible god. He loved this thing over any other things. Contrarily of what the majority of you believe, this man was not chosen! Are you surprised? How many of you have always believed that this man was chosen? How many of you always believed that the great flood was only a fairy tale imagined to put asleep children? In all truth, if I was in your shoes, I wouldn't believe it either. The story of the great flood stands in improbabilities, but then again! Sitting here on my ice field, I can see the probability of such a thing happening is real, and I the same time, uncertain. I have noticed for some time now, that the ice field was vanishing more quickly. That the season of cold and ice were shorter than it used to. I don't know why this is happening in this era… I have noticed it, that's all.

To come back to my savior with a white mane, do you still believe he was chosen? No, He wasn't. Then, how come this invisible god had confided him the mission to build a vessel in the middle of nowhere. To take aboard all the animals this vessel could contain? Like I already mentioned, he loved that god more than anything. This created the necessary predispositions to hear it. It is has simple has this. At the beginning, he doubted. He taught that he had auditee hallucinations. He clearly heard what was asked of him, but he didn't know what to make out of it, what it could be used for. He hesitated to talk to his pears about it. He attempted many times to talk about it, but has soon that he opened his mouth with the intention of telling the others of what he heard and felt in the deep of his being, he changed mind. He feared of being taken for a fool. He resisted to execute what these murmur was asking of him. He didn't know how he could, by himself, build such a big vessel. Where would he find the necessary materials to build it? Of how much time did he disposed of? He ignored it.

One morning, when the sun rose, He took the firm decision to execute what the murmur suggested him to do. He decided of the place where the vessel would take form, gathered all the money and material that he disposed of and started the construction of the enormous vessel. He began to trace on the rocky soil, the dimensions that the vessel would have, by its width and length. His family risked to ask him what he was drawing on the soil. The man answered that he was amusing himself by imagining the construction of a vessel on which he would board up some animals to create the first floating zoo. They all looked at him incredulously.

That night, while he was preparing himself to go to bed with his wife, she asked him where he got this crazy and surprising idea of building a floating zoo. She didn't recognize him. He, who had, all of his life, had been a humble person without any dreams of greatness, for sure a man of hearth, but without any ambitions. He looked at his wife and said:

— My wife, my love, unfortunately, I can't reveal the source of my inspirations. If I risk myself to unveil it to you, you will think that I am crazy and senile.

— Man of my life, father of our children, I have always known you has a reasonable and generous man. To see you with tears in your eyes, it is obvious that your project hides something that saddens you. Has you know, I am still your spouse, and we always leaned on each other in life ordeals. You can confide yourself to me, so I could bring you the help that you seem to need.

It is then that he told the love of his life: the whispers he heard that were more and more insistent. He explained to her that he had attempted to ignore what these voices were asking from him but without success. Has soon has he had started the first designs of what would become the refuge to save the animals of the improbable water flood, the voices that he heard, left to make place to the necessary inspiration to build a vessel of proportion never seen before. His wife listens attentively and took him in her woman's harm and said:

— If you want, I can help you to build this vessel. I am ready to back you up, whatever happens, I will always be at your side.

That night, they both fell asleep enlaced like lovers of the first days.

The following months, they had succeeded to build, by themselves, the bottom of the ship. He wasn't familiar with this kind of entrepreneurship, so the man with the white mane consulted naval architects and wood workers to take his divine mission forward. Has the ship been taking shape; a lot of humans mocked them and fed sarcastic remarks more offending from one to another. Their sons attempted to dissuade them to pursue, explaining that they were the laugh of the city. They couldn't support the stupid remarks made at their behalf anymore. It is then that my savior from the great flood and his wife told their sons where this crazy idea to build a floating zoo came from. They listened with attention, stupefied and stunned. When they were both done, their sons looked at each other without saying any words and all stood up has one. Then the oldest said:

— Mother and father, I think that you are both crazy, but your craziness is sublime and inspiring. In my name, and in the name of my brothers, permit us to help and support you to bring at term your crazy mission.

The following months and years were full of joy and promises. They all work at the same goal: building the ship. All the spare time that their sons disposed of were put to contribution. They had even partly demolished the sheds that protect their sheep's. They only left the roof to protect them from the bad weather. All the other habitants of the city laughed at them. Thinking that this foolishness was contagious they stood away from this illuminated family. After years of labor, the ship was almost done. All that was missing is the bitumen that would keep the ship leak less and dry.

It is at that precise moment that the rain started to fall like carpenters' nails. The man with the white mane gathered his family and gave the last necessary instruction so they could finish the works in his absence. The man kissed his wife and rushed to pack food for the trip that would take him to the great city. The hope to deliver the animals from the zoological park animated him. On in his pathway, he crossed humans panicking by this incredible water flood that didn't ceased to rise up the river waters, taking with her, the possessions and materials of people living in cities and villages that our savior went through.

After ten days of walk, he arrived at the zoo to choose the animals: one female and one male of each species. He selected them by their age and health. He would have liked to save them all, but the dimension of the ship didn't permit him to take on its board more than a couple of each species. He felt much sadness for the animals that he had to leave behind, the unchosen ones. After he selected the couples, he filled his lungs with air and shouted a word that reverberated like an echo in a rocky valley. The unchosen ones started to roar, to growl, to grunt and kick, and they all escaped from their prisons that were left open by our savior. It is then that he spoked to us, the chosen ones, in a language that we had never heard before, in such a way that it resonated in our wild hearths. We all gathered behind the man and began our long and silent walk in the direction of the ship. We walked in a file through mounts and valleys. We were the hope. We were those who would repopulate on unknown land the paradise of the first days of creation. This long walk went on for weeks, amongst which we witnessed an unimaginable thing. The waters covered the totality of the prairies; only some mounts and mountains resisted to the flood, but still, we saw gigantic rocks detached from them by the erosion of the torrential rain. The smaller animals climbed on the back of the bigger ones to prevent themselves from drowning. Finally, we arrived at the ship. The sons of the man came to us and were stupefied to see their father followed by all these animals. Exhausted, our savior fell on his knees. His sons rushed to hold him up; his legs couldn't support him anymore. In a weakened tone of voice, he ordered all the animals to get onto the floating vehicle. Once inside, the wife and daughters in law of the man took charge. They pointed out our paddocks that would become our refuge for the long months to come. Once all the animals were installed in their refuge, the family of our savior with the white mane took in the boarding board, and refuge themselves, like us, inside the ship.

Three days later, the ship started to flow in perfect equilibrium on the waters. We could hear the wood boards of the ship cracking by the lifting of the ship and also by the enormous weight of its cargo. We were all very tired and the rain was still pouring. The waters rocked the ship of the survivors of the flood, who all fell into a deep sleep.

After a few weeks, the rain stopped. All the passengers of the vessel woke up, yawned and stretched has much has they could in their small shelters. We were all very hungry. The white mane man had taken care of noting on the walls of each shelter of the different animals, the kind of food they ate so we could survive. Some were fed with straw and vegetables; the carnivores ate meat that came from the sons of the man's herd. Others received fish and some little creatures to feed those who only ate living prey. All of these tasks represented an incredible challenge for the humans, who relentlessly worked from dawn to dusk. They were busy feeding us, clean our spaces, and to take us out on the ships bridge so we could stretch our legs. To inhale fresh air did a lot of good. They took care of us that way for months and months, till the day we berthed on rocky soils. The day we landed will be printed for ever in my most precious memories. That day, all the animals and humans were asleep when a great sound woke us up. I and my female looked at each other worried. There was in the air a soft perfume that I didn't recognised: An aroma of liberty mixed with anguish and excitation. A moment later, our white mane savior came to see all the animals, one after the others, repeating these words:

— We finally arrived on the land of hope and renewal!

He had a radius smile, and I could see a luminous golden halo surrounding his body. We were all happy that the voyage had come to an end; all these months of floating on uncertainty and the unknown were finally over. The sons of the man installed the boarding board and we all started to board out and off the ship breathing in the perfume of the mountains. The white mane man repeated to every one of us that we were all free to live our lives and to multiply to insure the posterity of the animals' reign.

This is how all the animals got saved from the great water flood. Do you still believe this story is a fable?

****

This is a really nice story, but you still didn't explain how come you can talk with the humans.

— Right. I was getting to that. While we were preparing ourselves to walk off the ship, we could smell the mountains perfumes. There was something magical in the air. I was euphoric! The humans were shoving us to get out. My turn to get out came; I finally saw the light of day. There were no more clouds. The sun shined so brightly it blinded me. I had tears in my eyes because of it. While I engaged to descent the foot bridge, I stood up on my two back legs so I could swipe my eyes with my two front legs, and it is then I had an accident,

— An accident?

— Yes, an accident. You see little penguin, while I was all the way up there on the foot bridge standing on my two back legs swiping my eyes, I walked off the center of the footbridge. It is then that I stepped into thin air and fell some 30 feet down. I crashed my head on a big rock and I fainted. I regained consciousness moments later. I had blood running on my forehead. I was still a little bit stunned when I heard a voice coming from the ship. There was the white mane man calling me:

— Hey you! Down there… what are you doing there?

I couldn't believe my ears: I understood every word he said.

— Again, he said:

— Stay where you are, I'm coming down to join you.

I was still stunned when he arrived by my side. He shredded à piece of his clothe to swipe the blood off my face and said:

— Who are you? How did you arrive here?

— I was walking off the ship like the others and stood off the ramp and broke my head on a rock.

— You walked off the ship with the others?

— Yes! I walked off with my female polar bear when I stood out the board and…

— You are the male polar bear?

— Of course I am! You even freed us all to save us from the water flood.

The man cried and took me in his arms, telling me that a miraculous phenomenon just happened. He felt that I was a polar bear, but when he looked at me he saw and heard a human being.

— You understand little penguin? By breaking my head, a phenomenon that I can't explain, made in sort that humans saw me like one of their own. For them, I was a man, but for the animals, I was still a polar bear.

— It is difficult to believe. How can such a thing manifest itself? You have to admit this story is unbelievable.

— I understand you little penguin. It is true that this story is unbelievable, but the great flood really happened and we were all saved by the white mane man some thirteen thousand years ago. The story of the great flood is written in the humans' books. It is the truth.

— It isn't the story of the great flood that is difficult to believe, it is the fact that you can talk with the humans! Only by breaking your skull on a rock? You have to admit this is difficult to believe.

— I know, but then again, that is what really happened. After the accident, the man and his family took care of me, and let the time for my wound to heal. The sons of the man didn't understand how such a big person like me could have hidden on the ship without them noticing me. He explained to them that I was in fact the male polar bear, that I had an accident and by some unexplained prodigy, humans saw me has a man.

— What did you do afterward?

— I rejoined my female and walked for weeks. We found a cave to live in, in which, we believed that we were going to pass the rest of our days.

— Now that you have told me the story of your accident that seemed to have given you the power to look like a human when you are amongst them, how do you explain the fact that you are thirteen thousands years old?

— The accident didn't only given me the power to look like a human, but also to live eternally. In my case, the natural aging seems to have no grab on me. This is what I realize after living some thirty years with my female.

— Tell me, what happened next.

— Like I was telling you, my female and I found a cave to stay and to live in for the rest of our lives. We had a great desire to have cubs like our savior told us to, but without any success. Years after years, I saw my female aging, while my body didn't seem to gain any age since the day of the accident. One day, while I was out the cave picking up fruits of all kinds, I heard a scream coming from our cave. I rushed in: My female was dying. Shrivel up on herself she suffered greatly. I didn't know what to do to soften her sufferings. I hold her in my paws, and rocked her till her last breath, whispering in her ear that I love her and that I always loved her and that I couldn't wish for a better life partner, that she was a gift of joy and happiness in my life. After a couple of hours, she died, leaving emptiness in my heart and soul. I cried for a long time. Even these some of thirteen thousands of years after her death, I still think of her.

Listening to this story, the little penguin had tears in his eyes. The bear continued to walk in silence, remembering the happy days he had with his female companion of the great flood.

After a moment, the bear stopped, kneeled, and significate to the penguin to get down his back.

— Here we are, we arrived.

— You live here? What is this thing?

— This thing is called an igloo. I build it with my own paws.

— How bizarre! I never saw such a thing. You build it yourself?

— Yes. It is the humans of this country who thought me to build an igloo. Isn't it nice?

— Can I get in?

— I was going to offer it to you. Come, follow me.

— Bear, my friend, I am a bit tired and my belly is hurting, I would like to lie down and sleep.

— I am also tired, let sleep, and when we will wake up, we will go fishing.

They looked at each other, yawned at the same time which made them smile. They rolled their body in a ball shape and fell to sleep right away. The following day, the little penguin woke up and noticed that the bear wasn't there. He taught of the story that his new friend told the night before. « What an incredible story! A polar bear that talks with humans and builds houses like humans! The legend seems real: This animal really exists… and I slept in his home! ».

While the little penguin was still in his taught, the bear put his head inside the igloo and said:

— Good morning mister penguin! Slept well? Follow me, I need your help. I found a hole in the ice field but I am too big to slide in. It is you who will go into the hole and bring our lunch.

The little penguin followed him. Once near the hole, he slides in and brought fishes one at the time. They were big fishes. The bear was surprise by the ability of his friend. After the penguin had caught some fishes, the bear told him that they had more than enough to fill their belly. They sat side by side, like old friends and enjoyed their fishes. Whit his mouth full the little penguin said:

— I really liked the story that you told me yesterday. I didn't know that humans had their god.

— Of course they have one! What did you think?

— I don't know. I only know the god of the penguins… the invisible god of the penguins.

— It is the same than the humans. Sometimes I ask myself if it isn't the only thing there is… only god. Would you like me to tell you my following adventures amongst humans?

While the little penguin had still a piece of fish in his mouth, he said yes by shaking his head up and down.

— Where was I? Oh yes! After my female died, I dig an immense hole in the ground outside the cave and buried her. I founded myself alone for the first time of my life. If you only knew how sad I was little penguin! I didn't eat no more. I didn't know what would happen of me. No cubs, no female to share my life with… I was sad of my fate. After some years of living like a hermit, I decided to leave the cave. The waters that covered the plains and prairies were gone. I have traveled onto unknown lands. Sometimes I stopped and made home for some times. I nourished myself with fishes, with some little critters, and fruits hanging on trees. I covered earth this way for hundreds of years. I did, from time to time, cross the path of animals that had, just like me, survived the great flood, but they weren't the same: They were their descendants. For them, the story of the great flood was only a fantasy to put the children to sleep. I attempted to explain to them that this story was a true and real, and that I had made the trip with their ancestors. They all mocked me, treating me of old foul, adding that no animals could live for hundreds of years.

— Haven't you attempt to come back here, in the country of the polar bears.

— Of course I tried! But I didn't know which way to go. I sometimes asked other animals that I cross path, if they knew a country of cold, snow and ice. None of them had ever heard of such a place, even some humans that I crossed path with ignored the existence of it.

— You must of have felt alone…

— Yes! A great solitude, but I didn't give up hope, even if I didn't know when I would found my country. I have lived like a vagrant for more than two thousand years. What I didn't know at that time is that the water flood melted the ice of my country, of my birth. This is one of the reasons why I couldn't find it.

— What have you done after living like a vagrant for more than two thousand years?

— I am happy little penguin, happy that you are listening. After these two thousand years of wandering, I decided that it was time for me to change my life. I still didn't know how much time I had to live, but I seemed eternal. I often wished to die and join my female in the bear paradise. I prayed and wished a thousand times to die so I could see her back and give her a hug. Like I mentioned earlier, one day I took the decision that is was time to change my life. So I left, searching for that change, without knowing what was awaiting for me. After a few months, I met some humans who were traveling like I was. I ask them where they were going to. They then told me that they were going to the city of the stone carvers. I ask them if I could go with them. They said yes, that I was welcome, and there was work for everybody in this city. When we arrived, they took charge of us and thought us the trade of the stone cutters and carvers.

— Why did you have to cut and carve stones?

— To build the pyramids in the country of the pharaohs.

— Pharaohs? What is that?

— Nowadays, they don't exist anymore, but in this era, they were the sovereign of a magnificent country. It is for them that we carved and cut stones. Afterward, these same stones were transported on ships which travelled to the pharaohs' country. Then they were installed on top of each other to build the pyramids. You understand?

— I am not sure of understanding all, but please continue.

— By working hard and with some apprenticeship beside the masters' stone cutters, I became a good sculptor and made money out of it. I succeeded to integrate myself amongst humans and lived like them. I even had a little house that I had built my self from the leftovers of the stones that were then used to build the pyramids. One of the workers, with whom I worked, has even given me the permission to marry his daughter. She was a kind and loving person, with a great intelligence. We tried to have children, but without success. One day, they had the opportunity to make the trip all the way to the pharaohs' country. They said that I was sufficiently a good stone cutter to lead à fistful of workers who adjusted the stones on top of each other. So I left on the ship which transported the stones. When I arrived to destination, I was turned upside down by the view of those immense things.

— What have you seen?

— Little penguin, you won't believe me. I have seen this pyramid with my own eyes. It was enormous! Tens of times bigger then the vessel of the great water flood! There were thousands of people working to build it. There also were tens of ships arriving from everywhere, which carried workers, wood, clothing materials, food, and stone blocs. I had never been in my life a witness of such a thing. It was staggering! There were humans of all races: Some had white skin, others were ebony. They came from countries that were unknown from me. We were all there reunited to build the great pyramid.

— How long have you stayed in this country?

— Thousands of years! Till the day of the worker's liberation.

— The liberation of the workers? They were prisoners?

— No… not really. They had become the slaves of a tyrannical pharaoh, despotic, cruel and full of pride. I absolutely have to tell you the story of the liberation of the workers. It is extraordinary…

The prince liberator of the slaves

Moses

Of all man of exception that I cross path with while I was still in quest of my country of origins, the prince of slaves was the one I knew the less, but the last weeks that I spent with the people informed me a great deal on the conditions of the men slaves. Do you know what he did for the people? Did you know that the only thing we wished for was to treat the artists and workers with respect and decency? That he couldn't support despotic tyrants? This is why he joined the people. He preferred to stand on their side than being on the side of the tyrants full of themselves and who had no consideration for the workers. Those despotic pharaohs believe they were gods. This is why they built temples and statues to their images. In past times, these pharaohs were respected humans from the workers. They had a god which enlightened everything, just like the sun rise which hunts the obscurity of the night. They instilled us the belief from which we all had a bright and shining sun inside of us that enlightened our lives. For me, the only sun I knew was the one who made me sweat, but I taught that the idea of a shining sun inside of us was really amusing. Unfortunately, in a short period of time, it all changed: This once great nation became the pale shadow of what I had known thousands of years before, when all the people admired the kings. I remember a particularly dazzling and marvelous king who vowed an unconditional love for all life. He had known death and came back. This voyage in the other world had enlightened him. He said that he saw such an intense light, that it enlightened everything.

This nation of the inner sun that I had known was now a thing of the past. This nation had broken their sane spirituality that linked their life to their inside sun. This nation had become greedy of power, was one of a contemptuous pride. The pharaohs believed they were supreme divinities. They even pushed the audacity to order the people to idol them. Because of all this, the workers and craftsmen became slaves, and having nowhere else to go, they sank in the indifference of the domination exert by the pharaohs.

I had resigned myself to live this way for ever. To build pyramids for kings who transgressed human dignity, by ordering the building site masters to do better and faster than their predecessors, putting in peril the life and health of thousands of workers. I saw workers dying at work, crushed under the weight of enormous stones, and also craftsmen strangled by ropes poorly attached, but nobody cared. When a worker or craftsman died, we dragged his mutilated body out of the way, and life went on like nothing ever happened. The kings didn't only demand to work like slaves, but those who didn't work has hard as they could were threatened or hit with a whip. I have whipped workers out of breath and who were most of all, badly fed and sheltered. I royally couldn't care less; I executed the order, that's all. There was from time to time, few workers who rebelled of their conditions, but those were isolated and dragged in a public place and put to death in front of the others.

They were an example for all those who dared to rebel.

One night, as I was walking amongst the sleeping slaves; I've heard crying and sobs coming from the desert. I often heard workers complain while I was on night watch, but this sadness was something else, something I had never witnessed. It seemed to be coming out of a desperate soul. I was intrigued. Who could cry like this in the desert? I walked towards that sadness that made my hearth of ice melt. I then saw a man with his arms lifted up imploring the sky to give him the strength, the courage and the necessary inspiration to free the people who became slaves. By seeing him that way, I got closer to try to give him the help he seemed to need and also to attempt to console him. He was such a pity to watch that my hearth of ice turned into snow slush. As I was getting closer, he fell, face down to the ground, immobile. No more complaints came out of him that a couple of seconds before cut the night. After seeing him fell face down on the sand, I tried to precipitate myself to help him up and take him in my bear arms, but curiously, I couldn't move; my legs were welded to the ground. I looked at the lifeless man and slowly I saw an incredible glowing light that seemed of springing out of him, of his body. The more I focused on him, the more the light was growing, in such a way, that I now only saw the light. I didn't see the prince of the slaves lying on the ground anymore. I then felt in my being, a sudden and incomparable plenitude… an absolute plenitude. I then felt a compassion and love that was not of this world. I suddenly was stroke by dizziness and lost consciousness.

The next day, when I woke up, I had difficulty to open my eyes and I ask myself what I was doing there, on the sand. I had difficulty to remember what happened the night before. I had that curious memory of a radiant white light, but I taught to myself that it was only a dream, nothing more. So I returned to my guarding post like I normally did. A few days after this luminous dream, I've noticed that the workers and craftsmen were more docile and calm. I didn't need to use the whip on their back anymore. They whisper between them the name of a man and said they were all going to be free of their slave condition. I tried to know more from these rumors, but when I questioned my men about it, they all looked at me and said nothing.

The days past by and I felt something different in the air: Something had changed. The men that I bossed around were feverish and excited, but I couldn't determine the source. The following strange changing days, an inexplicable thing manifests itself right in front of me. I saw the see waters become has red has my blood that runs through my veins. I didn't understand. How the water could color itself that way? By this prodigy, all the workers stop working. They all rushed to the see to admire this phe-nomenon. They all kneel down and started to pray a divinity I didn't know. The building sites were in total stop. I was stunned! I had never in my life been the witness of such a thing. I grabbed my legs onto my shoulders and ran to the camps of the architects and engineers of the building sites.   They informed us that the construction of the pyramids were suspended for a few days, that we had to report ourselves to our superiors, and that they would inform us, every day of the new directives we had to follow and also, to stop whipping the workers immediately. In a few thousands of years by living in the pharaoh's country, I had never seen the building sites in a total stop; this says it all!

I returned to my men. They were talking between them of a man and a divinity unknown to me. I got closer to hear what they were talking about. One of them said that there was a man issued from the people and known by the royalties had soaked the tip of a wooden stick in the sea that became red as blood. They all said that they were all be free soon from the yoke of the tyrants. By hearing this, I thought of the dream that I had a couple of weeks before. The dream in which I saw a man crying in the desert followed by this light that seemed to come out of him. In fact… was it a dream?

The next day, I presented myself to my superior, like we were asked to. We were about twenty men waiting for his directives and orders. While I was waiting in line with the others, I told them what I had heard and learned from my men. They looked at each other and said that they had heard the same thing. Finally, our superior came out of his tent and told us to go back to our men and to only come back in three days. So I went back close to my men, without knowing when the works would start back. I seriously began to question myself on the man with his wooden stick and also on the divinity that seemed to accompany him.

That night, I had a bizarre dream, a dream of a sublime clarity. I saw myself leaving my body and afterwards, to elevate myself in skies of troubling truth. Radiant and loving skies, disarming and without frontiers. This sky was love. Everything I touched and saw was sweating out love, the absolute.

When I woke up the following morning my eyes were leaking with tears. I breathe in air profoundly to shake myself out of my emotions and looked around me. I noticed that something had changed but I couldn't explain it. I didn't see things the same way: I felt a profound love for all things, a great love for life. I presented myself to my workers to let them know of the directives I received the day before. One of them said:

— If we don't work, what are we going to eat? You know that we are fed only if we work! What are we going to eat?

It is then that I understood the serious and dramatic slavery in which the workers were held prisoners. How come I didn't understand this before this day? How did I become so insensible to their conditions? To answer this man that had suddenly opened my eyes, I said:

— I am on guard tonight, and I have the absolute liberty to patrol on all construction sites. I will come back amongst you with fishes and bread.

The following night, while I was patrolling and watching the sleeping slaves, I slowly walk towards the camps of the architects and engineers. When I got near the big tent where they had their lunches, I went inside. I saw on the big table fishes of all kind, bread, wine and water. I took the biggest fish and two breads. Suddenly I was taken by panic. I imagined that when the sun would rise up the next day, the chiefs of the construction sites would notice the absence of the big fish and would certainly investigate on its disappearance. That they would inform themselves to know who was on guard the night before and they would all point in my direction. I couldn't take that risk. I remembered a man who had the same job than mine. He got caught stealing bits and pieces that had fallen from the table and he was severely reprimanded. The chiefs had demoted him from his guard job and sent him to work with the slaves. I couldn't take that risk… how was I going to do? Suddenly, an idea came up in my mind! I began to pull out the meat of the big fish all the way to its bones. I deposit the meat in a table cloth and got out of the tent with the meat and the fish bones. Then I went to the tent of an architect renowned for his profound sleep and sleepwalk. I got in and deposit the fish bones on the ground by about a legs length from his bed. Then I deposit some meat crumbs on his pillow and ran out in a hurry. By proceeding this way, no one would suspect me. I was really proud of my subterfuge. Some instants later, I was at the camps of my men. I woke them up and showed them my loot and they all jumped in to treat themselves. I advised them to talk of this to no one, because if they did, I would probably lose my job and that we were all going to be executed on the public place to give us has an example to the others. None of us ever whispered a word about it. After this night, we all became accomplices… brothers.

Two days later, I presented myself at the tent of the architects and engineers, like we were ordered to. They informed us that the works would start back the next day, that all the construction sites would be reopened and that we all had to be in are post by sunrise. After receiving my orders, I walked towards my men to tell them that we would start working again. While I was walking I saw the skies became shadowy. I looked up to see the clouds that were passing in front of the sun; those weren't clouds; it was something else. I had never seen something like it! These clouds seemed to come down on us and emitted a buzzing sound. It is at this precise moment that I saw what it was: Millions of grasshoppers came down from the sky. They came from everywhere! I ran to protect myself and found refuge under a turned upside down rowboat for repairs. I putted my front paws on my ears and rolled myself in a ball to protect myself the best I could against this hallucinating invasion.

After about one hour, the insects left has they came. Getting out under my improvised shelter, I saw the destructive ravages from this armada that came from the skies. There was nothing left from the harvest. Everything had been eaten by the critters. I then knew it was time for me to change my life.

The following days and weeks convinced me without any shadow of a doubt that I had to leave this country and to never come back. I witnessed things that was has incredible than the see water becoming has red has blood and the invasion of the grasshoppers. I saw children dying of a mysterious disease; a rain of fire and ice falling from the sky; the see splitting in two so the slaves could cross it. I never been able to explain all those mysteries, but I know that the man and the god that seemed to accompany him everywhere had to do something with it. This is how the slaves obtained their liberty.

The little penguin, taken aback, then said:

— He did what? Split the see in two.

— Incredible, isn't it? Then again, that is what he did with the help of this invisible god. I would have never believed in it its possibility if I hadn't been an eyewitness of such a prodigy. He had ordered us to follow him to the Promised Land saying that we were all going to be freed. We followed him by the thousands. When we arrived at the sea, we ask ourselves how we were going to get on the other side. There were no boats to transport us. How would we do it? The prince climbed on a big rock, turned facing the sea, and in a gracious gesture, ordered the see to split in two, creating a passage so we could all walk in the bottom of it. While I was walking at the bottom, I looked at the vertical water wall suspended in thin air like by magic. The water suspended in thin air reflected the image of all those who were crossing the passage. I got closer to this water wall and put my paw into it to realise that it really was water. How such a thing could be possible? I focus on the water wall and saw magnificent fishes swimming like nothing had happened. I saw there a sign! I plunged my legs in the water to attempt to catch has many fishes that I could. I was filling up the chariots of the slave and yelled at them: « Give me a helping hand! » I showed them the fishes, but the slaves seemed hypnotised! I succeeded to wake up a few, and together we filled five chariots of fishes. Once we had cross on the other side, the prince held his arms up an ordered the sea to close it self. I was a bit disappointed, because I found this way of fishing really amusing. I knew that I would never again see that kind of prodigy.

— This is a crazy story! How did the prince split the sea in two?

— Just like you little penguin, I often asked myself the same question, thousands of times. At this day, I still didn't elucidate this mystery. But I know that the princes' invisible god had something to do with it.

— Where did they go afterward? Did they establish themselves on the Promised Land like the prince predicted?

— Oh yes! You see little penguin, a lot of them believed they would establish themselves on an oasis of abundance and peace protected from the tyrants. They imagined themselves living in a country cut off from all the other nations that lives on this planet, finally, they found more than they wished for: they established themselves everywhere on earth, mixing themselves with all nations, building on all continents temples in which they could pray their invisible god. I also heard that some of them established themselves in a very old country after the Second World War, creating, this way, a country of their own.

— The Second World War! What is that?

— I will tell you this story latter on…

— Ok. What did you do afterwards?

— After the prince had closed the sea, he came to me and asked where I got all those fishes. I explained what I did while we were crossing the bottom of the sea. He looked at me with a large smile and gave me a tap on the shoulder in sign of appreciation. After tapping my shoulder, he looked at me in a curious way and asked me: « Who are you? Where are you from? » I told him to follow me, that I had something to tell him in private. I told him all: Where I was from and what I was in reality. After listening, he took me in his arms and told me that I had to leave, that my destiny wasn't amongst the liberated people. I told him I didn't know where to go, that I tried numerous times to find my country. I was in tears. I confessed that I had saw him alone one night imploring the invisible god and that I had saw a blinding light at the same place where he stood. He listened without saying any words. He stood up and pointed to the north. He ordered his men to give me fishes for the trip and shake my paw.

In a tone full of love and authority he said: « Go and may god be with you. »

After he said these words, I left alone, leaving behind me thousands of years of my life.

— You never saw him again?

— Yes I did saw him again, a couple of thousands of years later, in bizarre circumstances… I will tell you this story later on, if I may.

— Ok. What have you done after leaving the liberated people?

— I left in search of my country. I met from time to time some humans with whom I travelled a bit with, sharing food that we got here and there. We told each other story, we slept under the stars, and after some time, we split, following our own path. I lived that way for thousands of years. I was hopeless to find back my country of birth. One day, while I was walking in a profound valley, pursuing my quest to find back my country which I had difficulty remembering, I saw a plump man sitting on the edge of a marsh who seemed to talk alone. I slowly approached, and looked around if there wasn't another person to which he was talking to. I saw no one but him. I got even closer, to see to whom he was talking to when suddenly he said:

— Hey you! The big one! Come and join me!

I presented myself to him and ask him to whom he was speaking to moments earlier. It is then he opened his hands and saw a little green creature with long back legs, like the ones I saw invading the country of the pharaohs, but smaller. He then told me:

— I was talking to her. See how nice it is!

I told myself that he must be terribly lonesome to speak with this insignificant creature. He insisted:

— See how exceptional and nice it is!

Really! I saw nothing exceptional in this creature except maybe that it was of a repulsive ugliness. He then asks me:

— You, the big one, still didn't find what you are looking for?

I retort:

— What makes you believe that I am looking for something?

— I can see that you are not from here. When I look at you, I see a big animal with white hairs.

I was seized by surprise. How could he have known what I was in reality? I risked myself by asking.

— It is because I am illuminated. I see the sublime reality of this world.

I turned back to look right in his eyes and saw light emanating from him. He had piercing eyesight, full of compassion, like he could see through me. He had a smile that illuminated life itself. It moved me.

I unravelled everything of my too long life; that I was lost, that I couldn't find my country, and that I lost hope. I talked to him about my adventures with men who illuminated life like he did. He listened attentively, nodding his head in sign of understanding and comprehension. When I was done telling my stories, he stood up and asks me to follow him, that he had something to show me. We walked many days in which he told me extraordinary stories on humans. He explained to me the visible and the invisible; the prowess of the human taught; the reincarnation of humans till the day of their realisation. I didn't understand the principle of reincarnation after death. Me who seemed to be eternal, I couldn't imagine such a thing. After we crossed a small creek, I saw a thing that I haven't seen in thousands of years. I simply couldn't believe it! I scrubbed my eyes to assure myself it wasn't a mirage. My companion then said:

— Look how beautiful it is! Does it remind you of something?

The little penguin intrigued asks the bear: what was so beautiful? What have you seen?

— Penguin, this human gave me one of the most beautiful gifts: A thing that I didn't hope for anymore. What presented itself in front of my eyes awakened memories of my childhood. I cried and laugh, jumping of joy. I felt in me an emotion of such intensity that I fainted.

— Bear, my friend, what have you seen?

— Patience… I'm getting to it! When I regained consciousness, the plump one was holding my head in one hand and splashed my face with cold water with the other. I opened my eyes. He looked at me with a luminous smile; help me getting back on my legs, giving me a tap on my back shoulder and said:

— Hope you're not too much deceived?

I looked at those things that rose up in front of me. My thoughts were shoving in my mind. I had difficulty to breath. Once more my eyes flooded themselves with tears. I couldn't believe what I was seeing. I tried to catch my breath back, but I just couldn't. The plump one scrubbed both my shoulders so I could catch up my breath, but once again, I fainted.

— What have you seen? Ask again the little penguin.

— Be patient, I'm getting to it. While I was regaining consciousness, I heard the plump one complaining by saying:

— Hey the big one, wake up, I'm suffocating!

I had fallen on my back over the plump one with all my weight. I stood up slowly and took three long breaths to shake me out of the emotion. I now could contemplate more calmly the most splendid scene.

— Will you tell me, at last, what you have seen that was so staggering! Begged the penguin.

— Little penguin, there was in front of me, mountains of a majestic beauty. Guest what was on those mountains?

— I don't know. I imagine that you'll finally tell me! ...

— There was, on those mountains, snow! A lot of snow which I found back for the first time in nine thousand five hundred years. Can you imagine the shock I received? I didn't remember how beautiful they were. I looked at the illuminated one, grabbed him in my paws and licked his round face. He then said:

— You want to go?

I followed him right on the spot. We walked again for some days to get there, days in which he told me that in the past he contributed to build a school in these mountains. He also told me that he was on some sort of a mission that pushed him to travel everywhere. He dedicated his life teaching the visible and the invisible and also the true nature of things.

When we arrived at the foot of the mountains we started the ascension of one of them. I was getting closer to my dreams, to my desires. I felt the child in me waking up. I was in paradise, in the *nirvana* like my new friend said. Finally, I was there, my four paws in the snow! I rolled myself in it, put some in my ears, covering myself in it. My companion laughed and tapped his thigh. He was as happy as I was. He then said:

— Don't hold yourself back for me! Have fun!

It is then that I got on my back and started to slide down like crazy, stroking the snow with my front paws to go even faster. I growled my found back childhood with pleasure!

I loved this human: He gave me the greatest gift of all. He demonstrated that, in spite of my age, I was still a child. That night, we slept on our backs in the snow. Looking at the stars, he explained to me the universe, to the infinite small to the infinite grand. He taught me that there was no coincidence and that all life on this earth made an all in its totality…

The illuminated plump man

The Buddha

The first time I met this man, I was turned upside down by the compassion that emanated from him. He had a simple way of seeing the visible and the invisible. He was a brilliant man with a sense of humour that tickled your spirit, your soul. I followed this uncommon man everywhere he went. I followed him like his shadow for more than twenty years. Did I tell you the story of the gift he gave me? The snowy mountains that reminded me of my childhood? He was one of the rare humans to see my real nature. This is the reason why I followed him for so long: Because he saw me as I was. The first day we met, I thought he was a little bit crazy by the way he saw life and the way he was living it. With the passing years I understood that he was of a great simplicity. My ears rejoiced of the words that came out of his mouth. It was like if the sky above was speaking to you, comforting you. I learned a great deal from him and I still thank him for putting up with me for all those years. If you only knew how we felt in his presence! He was like a crystal, a jewel. He understood so well my nature that sometimes I wondered if he was like me… a polar bear. Many times I have heard him say that we were all united in the totality, that we weren't separated from each other and that all living things in the visible and invisible universe made an indivisible all. He repeated that all humans reincarnated endlessly till the day of their awakening, and following this awakening, they became entirely free spirits. Me who seemed to be eternal… I never understood anything about reincarnation. I asked myself what was the necessity for humans to die, to come back in another body to reborn, and after some time, die again. This didn't make any sense for me.

The plump man explained that I was a rare exception, that I had an incredible chance to be immortal, and that I was also privilege to be a polar bear walking amongst humans and to learn from them. I often asked him how he explained the fact that I seemed to be eternal. He always answered the same thing: After my accident, the little connections in my brains changed their course, and consequently, the thoughts of aging and death had no effect on me. He added that everything is between our two ears, in our thoughts. He told me that the accident wasn't a random thing, and that invisible world knew me, and that same invisible took me to him. The first time he saw me, he knew right away that he had to help me understood what I was and to accept my difference, adding endlessly that I was privileged.

He also told me how he succeeded to awaken, to become one and reach nirvana. The nirvana is that state of plenitude and supreme serenity in which everything is revealed to you. He never always had been that way: He searched for a long time with different masters and professors, the teachings that made him reborn to a greater reality, more enlightened, more righteous, and more loving.

I asked him at least a hundred times where this translucent light surrounding his body came from, and why I didn't see this same light on the other humans. He always answered the same thing: He was illuminated from his interior, and consequently, this light projected itself to the exterior. By this fact, his thoughts and his emotions were in perfect harmony. What he thought and what he felt was the same thing; he was not divided, he was one with himself, one with his inner sun. He also told me that all humans had that light surrounding their body, maybe less radiant than his, but they all possessed one. Not only they had that light, but it emitted variations of colors more or less different from one another. I talk to him about the country of the pharaoh kings and told him when I first arrived in this country, they had a belief by which we all possessed a sun that enlightened all life. I told him that I found the idea of the inner light really amusing, but I never understood that belief. He responded by saying that it wasn't a belief, that the inner sun was real. He explained to me that the great majority of humans turned, more or less, their back to it, and consequently, they only saw the shadow of themselves. He gave me the following example:

— Do you see the sun hooked in the sky above?

— Of course I see it.

— Turn your back to it and tell me what you see.

— I see the mountains, the creek, the forest, the birds…

— You see nothing else?

— No!

— Look at the ground and tell me what you see.

— Nothing… nothing but my shadow!

— Now turn back and look at the sun.

— It is difficult… it's too bright!

— You don't see your shadow anymore, don't you?

— How can I see my shadow? I have the sun in my face and it's burning my eyes!

— Stop looking at the sun… you understand now?

— No, I don't!

— We all have inside of us a sun that it's comparable at the one in the sky. Most humans have, more or less, their back turned to it, and by this fact, they only see the shadow of themselves. By only seeing their shadow, they project it on the other humans… you understand?

— Not really. I'm sorry, I still don't understand this belief of the inner sun… it seems so zany! If I really had this sun inside of me, it wouldn't take long before it fried my guts, doesn't it?

— No. Because this inner sun is not quite the same has the one you see in the sky. However, it emits as much clarity and warmth. All those who decide to face it and fusion with it are more enlightened and have a warmer hearth. It is from this light that I receive love for myself and also for humans. Being enlightened this way, I see more clearly in myself. So I can help humans to see more clearly inside of themselves and chase the shadows that obstruct their vision and undermine their life.

— I still don't understand… I know nothing of this, but I can see that you shine more than any other humans I ever met. Where ever your light comes from, I believe you and really would love to understand.

— Keep in mind what I explained to you about the inner sun, and one day you will understand. Do you remember the day we met; while I was holding a small frog in my hands and that I saw all its beauty and gentleness?

— Oh, yes! That insignificant ugly and repulsing creature… I always asked myself what you found so beautiful in this creature from the marsh.

— It's because a saw the nice colors radiating from it. If I didn't stop there to contemplate it and talk to it, we would have never met… you understand?

— I had never seen our random meeting that way. So, according to you, the frog was some sort of an excuse so we could meet and make acquaintance?

— It wasn't an excuse. Like I already told and taught you, there is no coincidence. I'm hungry… lets pick up some fruits.

I followed this uncommon man for more than twenty years. Everywhere he went he taught humans about life. He demonstrated with simple examples the importance to be happy. He explained that we were all the creators and co-creators of life… of our lives. That there was always a cause and consequences, to our thoughts, words and actions. That we were all attached to one another, that we weren't separated from one another. This is the kind of language that the plump illuminated one entertained. I never always understood everything he said or taught, but by the simple fact of being in his presence my life took an another turn. I will never forget him.

✳✳✳

The bear and the penguin stayed in silence looking at the horizon. Some moments later, the polar bear broke the silence:

— Do you know what I'm thinking about?

— No. What are you thinking about?

— Lets go slide on the snow, in memory of our childhood and also in the memory of the plump illuminated one.

— Good idea! It's been some moons now that I didn't do such a thing! Let's go!

They both went in the direction of a small snow slop known from the bear. They played like crazy to climb and slide, climb and slide again till exhaustion.

— So little penguin, did you have fun?

— Yes, a lot! I didn't remember how amusing it was to slide, to become a child again, to simply have fun!

— You see how simple it is? You understand what the illuminated plump one did for me? He gave me hope that someday I will find back the country of my childhood, the country of my birth.

— How long have you stayed with this human?

— Only for some years… twenty years at most. While I'm talking to you, there is still some schools who teaches the philosophy of the illuminated plump man. Some of these schools have more than two thousand years. I thank the skies that I knew the plump one while he was alive.

— He died?

— I don't know, I think he is, but I'm not sure.

— What have you done afterwards?

— Like I told you, after walking through many countries in his company, to follow him like his shadow, one day, I told him about my intention of leaving. I told him that it was time to find back my country of ice and snow. He took me in his arms taping my back with his hands telling me not to worry, that I will find it back. He wished that I stayed, but he understood my decision. So I said so long and left. A couple of years later, while I was sleeping, I dreamt of him. I saw him surrounded by a white luminescent light. He comforted me with his words saying to continue my path, that I was guided and loved.

— What have you done after dreaming of him?

— Nothing more than I was already doing. I had the impression that I was turning in rounds, like a cub bear that runs after his tail. Years after years, I saw the same landscape. I wasn't able to orient myself to the north. I got more hopeless when I crossed city and villages that I went through tens or hundreds of years past.

One day I noticed that I had some little wounds on my skin, under my fur. Weeks after weeks, they spread even more on my body. The irritation of these wounds was difficult to support. The humans that I cross path with ran away from me, like I was a horror. In spite all, I still followed my way. Then I crossed a city that I had never visited before, this city was like a fortress. There was all around it, walls that protect it from the sandy and dusty winds. I went through one of these doors that gave access inside the city. I heard people talking between themselves about a man that seems to heal humans from their illness.

So I went looking for this man so he could help me get rid of my wounds that drove me crazy. Some hours later, I saw this healing man who spoked to people who gathered around him. I got closer to hear what he was saying. He spoke about an invisible god who seemed to be everywhere and in everything, a god full of love. By his language he made me think of the prince of slave and of the illuminated plump man. When he was done talking to the humans that surrounded him, I presented myself to him and ask him if he could help me get rid of my wounds. He asked me:

— Do you really want to heal? Do you think that I am capable?

— I responded by the affirmative. At the same moment, he touched one of my paws and said:

— You are now healed.

He touched me again and asked:

— Who are you? Where do you come from?

I looked at him. His eyes expressed love. He illuminated from his inside to the outside; he shinned. I was speechless from his luminous beauty and this mutes me. He prayed me:

— Go and show yourself to the man of law over there, and tell what I have done. They will have a testimony. After that, come and join me.

So I went and showed myself to the men of law, like he asked me. They seemed all embarrassed of my testimony that I gave them on my spontaneous healing. After, I went back to the man with the healing hands.

— If I understand what your telling me, Interrupts the little penguin, this man simply touched you and your wounds disappeared like magic?

— Yes… like magic!

— How is this possible?

— I don't know. It's like the prince of slave when he split the sea in two… I never succeeded to elucidate these mysteries. Once again, this invisible god seemed to be responsible for it. If you permit me, let me continue my story…

The healer with magic hands

Jesus

What a man this human was! What a marvelous gift he had! Not only did he had the gift to heal sick persons by simply touch them with his hands. But he also could join people in the depth of their being to liberate their hearts of demons that were a nuisance to their emotional, mental and psychic health. I stop counting the number of time that I saw him, with my own eyes, heal his siblings. He was amazing, magnificent, prodigious, and had a heart full of love for everyone. I followed this man like he asked me to. Having nothing more interesting to do, I followed him to his last breath of life

Every time he healed a person, he talked about his god that was inside him and inside all of us, adding that he was one with his god. By his language he made me think of the plump illuminated one. Some time I ask myself if he could hear what we were thinking, the kind of mental reflexion that we had in our thoughts. He said that his god knew everything. Being one with his god, he also knew everything, because he wasn't separated from his god inside of him.

He was so known that hundreds of people followed him everywhere he went, asking him advice or asking him to relieve them from their sufferings. When he had enough of the crowed, he retrieved himself on a mountain with his trusty companions, which I was part of. I remember one time; he advised us that he was going in the desert alone for about forty days. We look at him walking away in the desert. He only took with him a blanket and water. Ten days later, I ask myself what he could be doing, alone in the desert. One night, I went in the desert and search for him. Remembering that he didn't bring any food, I prepared a bag full of bread, fishes, water and wine. I passed the three following days searching for him and yelling his name in the desert. The fourth day, my nose smelled his particular odour; He had a curious odour, like a mix of flowers and sky, he had a divine odour. I followed that smell, and a couple of hours later, I found him. He was looking at the horizon in front of him. I approached him slowly so I wouldn't disturb him in his contem-plation. He stood up straight and asks me:

— Why are you here? What do you want?

— I was worrying about you, and I got bored with your companions. Then, I remembered that you had no food. So I brought you some, so you could survive for your forty some days.

— You worry about me?

— Yes, I worry about you, because of what you told me the first days we met. Do you remember what you said?

— I asked you to follow me till the day I will be put to death.

— Why would someone want to kill you? You are so generous. You heal the sick and chase demons. You are more and more popular and people worships you.

— I know that I'm appreciated and worshiped, but you have to understand one thing: It is not everyone who appreciates me. Some of them are searching to get rid of me.

— Who wants to get rid of you? You have enemies?

— No, I don't have enemies. But again, there is some people who sees me has a threat, an irritant, because I jostle their beliefs and religious practices. I tell them great truths on their behalf, I unmask their hypocrisy and lies, and because of those, they wish to illuminate me.

— It is by them that you will be put to death?

— Yes.

— How can you be sure?

— Because I hear them plot against me. I detect it in their eyes and attitudes. And I know all the probabilities of my future, even the ones where I will be put to death. For the prophecy to accomplish itself, I will let my self be put to death.

— A prophecy? Which prophecy?

— An old prophecy. It is written; « He will live amongst them, accomplishing prodigies, but they won't see it that way and won't recognise him has a son of the living god. »

— Are you obligated to give life to this prophecy?

— No. I have no obligation towards no one or any prophecies. I am only faithful to the god who lives inside of me. My father and I are one. What this god asks me to accomplish, I will accomplish.

— Can you explain to me why you retired here for forty some days?

— To re-evaluate my choices. You see all those people who follow me? All the power I have over them?

— Of course I see it! What you do for them is tremendous. They love you a lot, you know?

— I know they love me, but they don't listen or understand nothing of what I tell or teach them.

— Of course they listen to you!

— Yes, they listen, but they hear nothing. Have you notice how dumbfounded they are when I do prodigies with my hands, how they ask for more and more? How many times have I told them that what I am they also are? That they are all gods and it is because of the living god in me that I'm capable of such prodigies.

— Numerous times! And it is always staggering to see you heal people with your hands and chase demons with your words!

— This is the reason why I retired alone in the desert. To re-evaluate my choices. I am greatly tempted by the power I have on them. I could ask them for anything and they would do it. I do not wish for this power, because it's an illusion. I simply wish for all of them to understand that the god that is inside of me is also inside of them, that they don't need my care to heal their illness. They only have to recognise that they are also sons and daughters of god and to stop doubting. No religious beliefs or dogmas can offer them the salvation they are looking for. They will find this redemption and this salvation in the recognition of their divine essence that is proper to every one of them and the same to every one of them.

— I know that you are saying the truth, even if I don't understand everything that you are saying about your god, the god by which you do all these prodigies. I would like so much to understand and help you.

— Now that I have told the reasons why I retired alone, I ask you to leave and let me alone and think of the choices that I have to make. I have to be alone for this.

— Do you want me to leave the food that I brought?

— No, and I thank you for it. You can bring it back with you. However, let me have the water, in case I would run short of it.

I left the man, leaving him alone with is inner god. He came back forty days later, a couple of weeks after I visited him. He was more luminous than ever. He shined like the sun; he was dazzling. I still followed him for some times, listening to every single word he spoked. The day he was put to death, I understood that he decided to stay faithful to his inner god. I cried his death for a long time. He will stay for ever in my most cherish memories.

***

The little penguin, sadden and incredulous of what he had heard, mumbled:

— You saw him die?

— Yes. I saw him die in atrocity. But before I tell you about his death, I have to tell you something incredible. Do you remember what I said earlier, about the prince of slaves, that I saw him back in bizarre circumstances?

— Yes, I remember! You told me that you saw him some thousands years later, I think.

— That's right. And it's in the company of the healer that I saw him. One night, his companions and I, followed him on a small mountain to hide away from the crowed that ask more and more healing prodigies from the healer. To get peace and quiet, we refuge ourselves on it. One night, while we were all asleep, I was awakened by words and by a strange glow that illuminated the night. I rubbed my eyes and saw the healer talking with two other men. One of these men was the prince of slaves. He wears some kind of a luminous rob. I rubbed my eyes again to assure myself that I wasn't dreaming… It was really him! I stood up and ran in his direction with the intention to jump in his arms and joyfully give him a hug or two. When I arrived near him I jumped to hug him, but I past right through him, like he wasn't there. I found myself face on the ground, surprised of what just happened. Before I had the time to stand up, the prince of slaves came to greet me. He was transparent, more luminous than the last time I saw him. He said to me:

— Go back to sleep, and forget of what you just saw. Don't talk to anyone about it.

He was still talking with love and authority. I executed what he asked, and went back to sleep.

— What did you do? Past through him?

— I concur, it is hard to believe, but that's what really happened to me. He was like a specter, a ghost, discussing of things and other with the healer and another ghostly friend that I didn't know anything about. The next day, I woke up, and went to see the man with prodigies to talk to him about my real nature and the fact that I had known one of the men he was talking with. He told me that he knew everything about me, and that I had to follow him till the day he would be put to death. Not understanding why, he was telling me this, I continued to follow him with his faithful companions. He always talked about his invisible god, everywhere he went. One night, while we were walking in a less crowded street, a woman came and took the healer into her humble house. After she closed the door, his traveling companions ask themselves what the healer could find in this woman recognised by all by being a woman of no great virtues, a prostitute. Ignoring their gossip, I went to lie down and sleep under a window of this woman's house. I heard some groan of love coming from the bedroom. This reminded me of the happy days I had lived with my female polar bear, and I fell asleep cradled by these soft memories.

— After all those millenniums, you were still thinking of her?

— Yes. But I wasn't suffering of her death anymore. The memories I had of her were soft and happy. Even if I had a few human females as companions of life, even if I loved them all, none of them could have taken her place. When I thought of her, she reminded me of my country of ice, the country of my childhood.

— What have you done afterwards?

— I continued to follow the healer like he asks me to, till the day he was put to death.

— How did he die?

— Nailed on a piece of wood rising from the soil, hands and feet nailed on it with long metal rods to support him. His death was an agonising one.

— Such a thing is not possible. Why the humans did that? What the healer done wrong?

— I have to explain something to you, little penguin. The humans are not like us. For an example, look at me: I am different from the other polar bears, I don't talk like they do. Never in their right minds would they get the idea to kill me because of the stories I'm telling them. In the worst cases, they yell out that I'm crazy and stay away from me, that's all. But humans don't behave the same way we do. If an individual says things that shatters or disrupts their beliefs, and these same new ideas contraries them, they will try anything to shut him up, even kill that individual if they have to. That is precisely what happened to the healer with magic hands.

— If what you are telling me is real, humans are more savages than I thought.

— You know what makes them so savages? Ignorance and stupidity. Most humans that I've known don't think by themselves, and don't act by themselves. They follow the masses without questioning why they do so. I'll give you a good example later on.

— I still don't understand what the healer with magic hands had done wrong to get killed.

— Like I just said, with his word and prodigies, the healer claimed has a fact that the invisible god that everybody talked about was within themselves and everywhere. At that time, the beliefs preached by the religious leaders stated that god was something uniquely outside of us… you understand?

— I'm not sure to understand. They killed him only for that?

— Yes, only for that. He was idolised by the masses, but was a major irritant for the political class that ruled this country. Those leaders kept the ignorant masses under unbearable religious laws that kept them from the liberty to think by themselves and other religious beliefs imposed since their tender childhood.

— I'm happy to be a penguin, I wouldn't want to live amongst humans, they are too dumb.

— You know; it wasn't all that bad. I had great moments of happiness amongst them.

— What have you done after the death of the healer with magic hands?

— While I was watching him die, he asks me to get closer, that he had something to tell me. So I approached him and then he said:

— Go north, you will find back your country.

— I couldn't believe my ears! With all the suffering that he was undergoing, he still wanted to help. I thanked him again to have healed me from my wounds. I promised him that I will never forget him, and that he will always be in my hearth. I left with tears in my eyes. I wished more than ever to find back my country of ice and snow. I had more than enough of the humans. I was fed up with them. Once again, I found myself alone. I didn't want to talk with humans which I crossed path with. I was discouraged by the human race. I had a grudge against this invisible god by creating me this way… I hated him. I turned round and round for hundreds of years, still not knowing to orient myself to the north.

One day, while I was walking in a desert of sand and rocks that seemed endless, I found a little pool of water surrounded with trees and shrubs. I stayed there for some times, to rest and fill back myself with energy. A couple of days later, men came mounted on horses and armed with long knife to do the same thing I was doing. To not being seen by them, I hid behind shrubs waiting for them to leave. I fell asleep and started to snored, which betrayed my presence. Men came to wake me up and ask what I was doing here. I answered that I didn't want to talk to them; all I wanted is for them to leave me in peace. They insisted for me to stand up and follow them. I told myself that once the presentation made they would leave me in peace. They brought me in front of a man that seemed to be their chief leader. The man looked at me from head to toe and said:

— You're the one who was snoring that way?

They all blast in laughter. Not giving a damn about them, I answered:

— Yes, it was me! Did I disturb you mister?

Surprised by my answer, he got closer and asked:

— What are you doing here alone?

I answered him with a dry tone:

— Mind your own business!

— Why were you so insolent with this man, replied the little penguin.

— Because they were disturbing me. I didn't want to be in the company of humans anymore, or to be seen has a human. After seeing the death of the healer, I wished only one thing: To find my country and becoming a polar bear again.

— But those humans were armed! Weren't you afraid that they might have killed you?

— I have to confess one thing, little penguin. I had more than enough of the humans, secretly, I wish I was dead. In all evidence, you can see that they didn't kill me.

— Yes evidently. But how did he react to your insolent answer? Did you fight?

— No! He got closer to me and said: « I like you. I like your attitude and I need man like yourself in my army. I wish that you come with us and astride by my side. » He bent his harm straight so we could shake hands. Not knowing how to respond to this friendly invitation, I also bent my harm straight. While my paw took contact with his hand, an extraordinary thing happened. I saw, coming out of the skies, a ray of dazzling and luminous white light that entered the head of the chief. His entire body illuminated itself. I felt this light passing through him, and the more the light past through him, the more he took roots into the ground. He sank in the sand to his ankles. I couldn't support more of this light, so I wanted him to let go of my paw, but his hand seemed welded to mine. With all my strength I tried to separate myself from his grip but without success. After a few seconds, he got his sense back and said:

— I know everything about you, and I wish to talk with you.

He got himself out of the sand in which he had sank, and ordered his men to wait for him, that we will be back in a couple of days. He packed some foods, water, a tent, and covers. He invited me to follow him into the desert.

A few hours later, we stopped and he invited me to talk about myself. I told him everything of my life: My meetings with humans that I had known and were invested, just like he was, by this light. He listened to all of my stories, I made him cry, I made him laugh. He saw me has I was. In his company, I gain confidence and hope. I talk to him this way for many days. After telling him everything about me, he reaches in his bag and gave me a book. I ask him what this book was about, He told me to just read it. I began to read it and it made me cried. I was so happy to read it.

— What was written in this book that made you cry of happiness? Ask the little penguin.

— Little penguin, of all things that I received in my life, this book was one of the most magnificent gifts. The more I flipped the pages, the more it amused me. This book was telling the stories of humans that I had known and other humans that I didn't know anything about. There was the story of the white mane man who saved the animals from the great flood, the prince who freed the slave people from the pharaohs, the human with magic hands who had healed me from my open wounds. I thanked him at least a hundred times for this gift and ask him what I could give him in return. He asks me to combat his enemies by his side that were trying to harm and kill him.

— Bear, my friend, why humans tried to kill him?

— For similar reasons of those by which they killed the healer with magic hands. For words and ideas, he knew as the truth which was the opposite of what was teached. According to him, there was only one god, without a name, like my friend the chief used to call him…

The enlighten chief

Muhamad

The first time I met this man, I almost fought with him. I was fine on my oasis when he came with his companions and disturbed my loneliness. After seeing the healer die in atrocity, I didn't want to live amongst humans anymore. All I wanted is to find back the country of my childhood and to never come back to what is called the civilised world. I questioned myself about this man for a long time. Where that light could come from? The light that entered the top of his head? How did he guess what I was? I knew that he wasn't like the other luminous humans that I had met in the past. Nevertheless, he also had a divine mission to accomplish, like the other humans that I had the privilege of meeting. A lot of people believed that he couldn't read and said he was illiterate. Maybe it was true. However, he seemed to know more than anyone else, understanding the sense and secrets behind the ancient texts. He knew the invisible god. He confides to me that he had saw some sort of angel or archangel which appeared from nowhere; His knowledge of the invisible gave him a lot of power on his siblings and he accepted all the responsibility that came with this power. Strangely, he made me think of the healer with magic hands. One time, when I was alone with him, he told me that contrarily to the healer; he had no prophecy to accomplish. However, he would defend his life against those who wished to hurt him. His only mission was to live according to the ancient texts. He made a lot of enemies because of his profound knowledge of the invisible and ancient texts. He turned upside down all the dogmas and beliefs of that era. He was radiant and truthful, simple and honest in his remarks. He never seeks to harm anyone. He knew and understood humans better than anyone else. It was essentially for this reason that I loved him: he was crystal clear.

For many years, I astride along with him to combat his enemies. He understood the men that were seeking to hurt him, he even loved them. In no occasion he let hatred penetrate his hearth. He often said to his men that hatred soiled the soul, and for this peace to come to you and in you, we should all keep our hearth pure. He often talked about the children, He made me noticed the simplicity and their joy of life. They were for him a great source of inspiration. Sometimes, he composed poems and tales for them. This exceptional human was great and amusing to hear.

I combated his enemies with ferocity, and defended the divine truth with hatred and rage in my hearth. I cut opposing warriors in two. I cut their head off, I impaled them, I burned them. I was blood thirsty. I was a monster.

I didn't like the enemies, and I didn't like my companions of war either. I hated all humans equally. I didn't want to live amongst the humans. When my friend the enlightened chief heard of what I was doing to the enemy, he convoked me to hear from my own mouth, if what the others were saying about the atrocities that I was committing against the enemy was true.

I was proud to tell him in details how I killed those men, how I disposed of their heads once I decapitated them of their body. The chief listened without saying anything. Once I finished telling about my carnages, he ordered me to follow him into the desert, that he had something to tell me in privacy. After a few hours, we stopped. While we were mounting our tents, he asks me:

— Are you well?

— Yes, marvellously well! Why do you ask?

— You don't ask me why I wanted to be alone with you.

— Not really. I imagine you wanted to be alone with me to give me a medal, and you didn't want to make the others jealous, so you dragged me here.

—No… I wish to talk to you about the invisible god who is in everything and everywhere.

— I don't give a damn about this invisible god! I don't understand this thing; I don't believe this god of love and light.

— You don't believe in the existence of this god?

— If your god really existed, he would have never let the healer with magic hands die on a piece of wood.

— You loved the healer?

— Yes, he was my friend. When I look at you, when I listen to you, I see him in you. It is like you were him, but different at the same time, I will let no one hurt you.

— You, who have known him while he was living, haven't you learn anything from him?

— I learned a lot of things from him, but what I remember the most, it's the stupidity of humans and their hypocrisy. I remember seeing with my own eyes, men and women that he had healed rejoice over his death.

— I understand you my friend. Now, depose your hand in mine and tell me what you feel?

— Nothing... I feel nothing. Oh, wait! I feel something... I feel uplifted... I feel weightless... I see a soft light... it's intensifying! Let go of my paw, please, let go my paw, I can't take it anymore!

When he let go of my paw, I was out of breath. Tears were flowing from my eyes. I look at the enlightened chief. He was there, more luminous than ever. He talked about his invisible god and explained how he started communicating with this thing; that he was divinely invested; That he had to obey to the revelations that he received from this invisible god, the out of name, like he called it. I listened to him and admired the light that came out from him. I was speechless; I couldn't speak anymore. I received his words like a soft music of harmonic melodies. After a few hours, I couldn't see his body anymore. I only saw that light that made him as bright as a thousand fires. Slowly, I fell in a profound sleep, cradled by the words of the enlightened chief and also by his god that inspired him. When I woke up, the chief had disappeared. Seeing him nowhere, I then understood he didn't want me in his army anymore. He left behind, a tent, a horse, some food, and a bag in which I found the book he gave me the first day we had met. I left that blond desert of sand to never come back again. Once again, I didn't know where to go. I didn't know either if I would found the country of my childhood, the paradise of my birth. At this precise moment in my life, I cared only for one and unique thing, and this thing was the happiness to love.

✳✳✳

Happiness, war and return

— So, you really fought the enemies? Ask the little penguin, fascinated.

— Yes. And the more we combat and won battles, the more his army grown. Sometimes, his companions reproached him loving the enemies has much has he loved his friends. Never had I heard him say any bad things on any one. He was humble and strong. He often prayed this invisible god in secret, far from anyone's indiscretion. He was a light for everyone and I loved him very much. After abandoning me in desert, he left a note saying that I had to forgive others, and forgive myself. After reading his note, I started to cry like a child. I was incapable to stop crying, and I cried every day for the following fifty years.

— Fifty years! You had a lot on your heart and soul!

— Oh, yes! I wasn't aware of all the hatred that I carried in me and all the atrocities that I committed in the name of that same hatred. I relearned to love and also to love that invisible god that seemed not wanting me in his paradise. Being incapable of finding my country of ice, I resigned myself to live amongst humans for ever.

— You had abandoned hope of finding the country of your childhood?

— Yes! I was happy of this abandon, because it made me love humans even more.

— Have you ever seen the chief again?

— No, I never seen the chief again in the flesh, but his extraordinary life has been immortalised in the humans' books. To this day, we still talk about him, and also all of those who enlightened life like he did.

— Where did you go after the chief had abandoned you in the desert?

— I left without any destination. The only thing that I desired and search for was happiness. I didn't want to fight anyone anymore: I simply wanted to live, that's all. I travelled and lived in magnificent cities and villages, where it was good to live in. I met thousands of humans, I got married tens of times, I practiced tens of different trades and I lived this way over a thousand years.

— Did you find happiness?

— Yes! Everywhere I went, happiness was there, because happiness was inside of me.

— Even if you had abandoned hope of finding back the country of your childhood and live amongst humans for ever, how did you find it, find the ice fields? You must have done something, right?

— Yes. But what follows is difficult for me to tell, because it's not that many years ago. But if you really want to know, I will tell you.

— I want to know! How did you do it?

— Some sixty or seventy years ago, while I was living in peace in a small village, we heard that the country in which I was living in, that part of it was under the control of the enemy. A lot of the villagers had left to join the army or the resistance of the country I was living in, to combat the enemy invaders, while others had decided to just leave the country. I didn't want any participation in this war. Others and has myself had decided to leave the country. So we all left in search of a country where there was no war. Everywhere we went, we met other humans that were also in search of a way to leave. After a few days, I separated myself from the group to try to find refuge alone. I finally found a little boat that transported its passengers in a country on the other side of the ocean. I gave to the captain of the boat all the money I had to have my place on this boat. We left the port a couple of days later. This crossing made me think of the one I had with the white mane man when the animals were saved from the great water flood. We were all piled up like cattle. While on the boat, I heard rumours of world war from which many nations were implicated and that people of the same origins were massacred in inhuman ways. All humans whom I made the crossing with feared for their life. I ask the captain who were those massacred people that everyone talked about. He told me that those massacred people lived in a country neighbour to the one that I had just left, and that the war king of this country gathered those people in slaughter houses to kill them by the thousands.

— Bear, my friend, who were those people? Why did that king wanted to kill them by the thousands?

— Those people were the descendant of the prince of slaves. This war king pretended that those people were responsible of the death of the healer with magic hands two thousand years ago, and those same people shouldn't be considered has humans, that they were an inferior race. I couldn't believe my ears! Do you remember what I told you early on little penguin? That human were capable of putting things in our brains and thoughts that had nothing to do with reality?

— Yes, you told me. It was in the era of the pharaohs' king, I think.

— That's right. This war king had so well succeeded that a lot of humans believed what he said. They executed tens of thousands of humans without asking any questions.

— I cannot believe what you're telling me. This is an unthinkable thing!

— Every thing I'm telling you is authentic and real. I already told you that humans don't think or act like us. Never animals like us would think of invading another species, more the less, eliminate them by the thousands… by millions.

— So you succeeded crossing the ocean, and that's how you came back?

— No! When we arrived in this northern country, there was snow everywhere and it was very cold. It looked like the country of my birth. The hope to find back what I had lost sprung back in me at the speed of light. The memories of my childhood rushed in my head; tears of happiness flooded my eyes. I danced and growled with joy! I ask some humans if they knew a country made of ice, a country populated with polar bears. They looked at me like if I was crazy. They answered that there was such a country, all I had to do was to walk straight to the north and I would find this country.

— So that is how you ended your adventures with the humans?

— No! The following nights, after I arrived in this northern country, I dreamt of the slave people and the thousands of years that I had lived amongst them. I dreamt of the pyramids, of the prince of slaves, of their sufferings that they endured, and also the slaughter house in which they were killed by the thousands. Those dreams were tormenting me; I woke up in sweat and trembling. I saw hundreds of men and women enrolled themselves in the army to free the occupied countries. I was sad for the people, for all people who fought. I had to do something for them. The following night, I dreamt of the prince of slaves. He was dressed of a dazzling light. He was accompanied of the healer with magic hands, by the plump illuminated one, by my savior with a white mane, and also by the enlightened chief. They all smiled at me and said in one voice:

— Go up north; your country is waiting for you. This war is not your war. Go home and don't worry for the humans. They will survive without you. Your adventures amongst humans are over.

I took them all in my paws; one after the other. Thanking them for everything they had done to help me, also helped the humans. I told them how lucky and happy I was to have known them, and that I missed them all.

— This is how your adventures with the humans ended and found back your country?

— No. The next morning, when I woke up, I took the decision to enrol myself in the army who had greeted me, to combat their enemies.

— But why? You didn't have to do that! Your luminous friends told you to leave and go up north and to not get involved in that war! Why have you done that?

— I had two excellent reasons to react this way! The first reason was that I taught I had a debt towards the people of the prince of slaves, the people who I whipped in the era of the pharaohs. The other reason was that I didn't want to be immortal anymore. I wanted to die. I had more than enough of the humans and their stupidity. I taught that it would be great to join with my luminous friends, somewhere in the heavens. Of all humans that I have known, these enlightened humans were a great source of hap-piness, because they saw me has I was, and they all gave me some of their light. If you only knew little penguin, what we feel when this light submerges us, you would have a better understanding of what I'm talking about.

Like I was saying, I enrolled myself in the army, where they taught us how to use a rifle gun and execute the order of our chief. After a few months of training, we all got aboard a war ship that took us in the country that I had just left a few months earlier to run away from that same war. We arrived a few weeks and disembark on a sandy beach. We were greeted by the enemy in a rain shower of projectiles that they shot us with. I saw my companions fell and die one after the other under this infernal burst of bullets. The enemy also trough at us little engines that exploded and decapitated in pieces all those who received it. I felt the rage rising up in me. I remembered of all the hatred I had in me when I was in the army of the enlightened chief. Rage was invading me. I did combat barbaric enemies in the past, but this war was different of everything that I had known. I felt the savage and wild animals that I was, growing up to the surface of my being. I deposed my artillery, I took my military clothing of my skin and I ran furiously in the direction of the enemy. I growled with all my might. I had only one desire, and this desire was to kill. My companions shouted at me to come back, that I was running to my death, but I didn't care anymore. I told myself that if I was going to die, I will die like a polar bear, in the skin of a polar bear. I succeeded to dodge all the bullets and projectiles all the way to the enemy. I took by surprise a first enemy. I took his neck in my mouth and bit him has strongly has I could. I felt his blood running on my tong. While he was still wriggling in my mouth, one of his companions surprised me. I growled in pure savagery and teared half its face off with my paw. He cried and shouted like a wounded animal, so I pulled his head off its neck so he would stop complaining. I continued to fight this way till they were all dead. I killed in all thirty-seven enemy soldiers.

When my companions joined me, I was in the middle of my lunch, quietly eating the guts of an enemy. When my companions had seen the carnage that I had done, some of them vomited everything they had in their stomach. Instead of congratulating me, they handcuffed me and took me back to the northern country. I was brought in a court of justice for crimes against humanity. During the trial, I attempted to explain to the judge of justice that I was in reality a polar bear that I was over thirteen thousand years old; that I didn't understood why I have been handcuffed after valiantly and courageously fought the enemy at the peril of my life.

— They put you in jail? Ask the little penguin incredulous.

— No. They took me in some sort of a hospital conceived for men and women who have ideas and behaviors judged inacceptable by the majority of humans. In other words, I was interned in a hospital for the mentally ill.

— But why?

— You see little penguin, when a country is in war with another, the soldiers of their army can kill the enemy with the weapons we give them. They can explode each other in thousands of little pieces. But they cannot run naked and break their necks by biting it, and eat them. This is what I have learned.

— So you were considered as crazy… a crackpot?

— Yes I was! And I liked it. I met in those walls very amusing people. There was a man who thought he was a fruit and past most if his time asking the other mentally sick to peal him. After some time, I got tired and bored with the fruit man. So I executed what he was asking for and pulled his cloth off. When I was done pulling his cloth off, he precipitated himself in the hall running everywhere shouting: « I got pealed... I got pealed! » The last thing I have heard about the fruit man is that he had curiously healed from his obsessional fixation of being a fruit. He was liberated and freed by a comity of brainy psy-chiatrists, who didn't understood what could of happened to the fruit man that healed him so suddenly and rapidly from his mania. I thought to myself that he only needed someone to peal him. That is what I had concluded. There was also another man, like myself, who had fought the enemy, and was also judged for crimes against humanity.

— What had he done?

— Nothing special... He went alone at night in enemy territory and pulled out their hair with a knife. He called that a scalp. This man quickly became my friend. He was intelligent and proud. He told me that he was the reincarnation of a great chief that occupied this country before it got invaded by the white man. I talked to him about me and of my too long life, of the enlightened being that I had known. He seemed more interested by the illuminated plump one, for whom reincarnation of the soul was a reality. He listened without judging me.

One day, He introduced me to a woman who worked in the hospital taking care of the sick and for whom he had a lot of love. I shook the hand of this woman and felt in me a soft light. I looked at her right in her eyes and saw that soft light irradiating from her. She was radiant. She told me that she knew everything about me, and this coming night, she would help us escape and that I had to go up north. That night, me and the reincarnated chief, escaped with the help of that generous and gentile woman. We walked for weeks together till we got to the village of his siblings. We were greeted like heroes. I pass some time in their company. One day, I advise the reincarnated chief that it was time for me to go back to my country. He took me in his arms and promised me that one of these days he would visit me. He gave me a little thing wrapped in a case that always pointed to the north. After months of walk I finally reached the ice fields. The emotions that I felt were choking me. I cried and laughed. I kissed the ice under my paws. And I continued my walk till I met other polar bears… that were running away from me.

— Why the other polar bears ran away from you, asked the little penguin?

— Because of my odour… I smelled like humans, I smelled like death. It took me seven years to get rid of that odour. One night, while I was asleep, a female polar bear came and lied down at my side. I woke up while she was licking my ears. I turned back to look into her soft and beautiful eyes, and then, I cracked up! After thirteen thousand and some few centuries wandering amongst humans, I had in front of me a splendid female that was offering herself to me! I took her like crazy. I copulated with her fifty-two times in a roll. We were exhausted but happy! After copulating this way, I had a stupid smile hook to my face for months.

— What an incredible life!

— Indeed… what a life! An incredible life and it's not over. I still have a lot of things to tell. I have learned so much from the illuminated humans that I met! One day I will wright some sort of a testament on the subject. I'll talk to you about it another time, Ok?

— Ok! Bear, my friend, I got to go. I have to go back to my country and find my siblings and testify of my adventure into the unknown and also of our meeting.

— I understand you, little penguin, but before I accompany you to the ocean, I want to show you something. Have you noticed that the season of the nights were close?

— Yes. That's why I got to go… to not be caught by the darkness of the long nights.

— Then, turned back and look at the skies. Have you ever seen an aurora borealis? Isn't it magnificent! When I look at these things, it is like I was seeing my illuminated friends, I see in these things all the love and compassion they expressed.

The bear deposed one paw on the little penguin shoulder and both look silently the spectacle of light deployed in the sky.

Post face

I still haven't told you why I have entitled this testament *whit out religions*. This is simple! After listening hundreds of times my illuminated friends tell me about their invisible god that seems to be everywhere and in everything, I came to the following question: From which religion is this invisible god? You don't know? Neither do I! If that god had some kind of a religion, my illuminated friends would have told me so… that is all!

The polar bear

danielstamour.com

www.ingramcontent.com/pod-product-compliance
Lightning Source LLC
LaVergne TN
LVHW041700190726
843493LV00007B/1882